THIS BOOK

C000142588

| Name: | | Age. |

| Favourite player: |

2020/2021

My Predictions...	Actual...

The Swans' final position:

The Swans' top scorer:

Championship winners:

Championship top scorer:

FA Cup winners:

EFL Cup winners:

Contributors: Sophie Davis, Chris Barney & Peter Rogers.

A TWOCAN PUBLICATION

©2020. Published by twocan under licence from Swansea City AFC.

ISBN 978-1-913362-35-5

PICTURE CREDITS:
Action Images, Athena Picture Agency and Press Association.

£9

CONTENT

FREDDIE 1 WOODMAN

POSITION: Goalkeeper   **DOB:** 04/03/1997
COUNTRY: England

Woodman joined the Swans on a season-long loan from Newcastle in August 2019 and quickly became a fan favourite among the Jack Army.

Throughout the season, Woodman made 43 appearances and saved three penalties out of the five he faced, in matches against Derby, Blackburn and Fulham. The former England youth international sealed another season-long loan in August 2020.

4 JOE RODON

POSITION: Defender   **DOB:** 22/10/1997
COUNTRY: Wales

Llangyfelach-born Rodon signed for the Swans as an eight-year-old and has since played an integral role in the heart of the Swans' defence.

Rodon had a lengthy spell on the sidelines last season due to injury but made 21 appearances for Steve Cooper's side in all competitions. He also made his international debut for Wales against Azerbaijan in September 2019.

MARC GUEHI 5

POSITION: Defender   **DOB:** 13/07/2000
COUNTRY: England

The centre-half initially joined Swansea on loan from Chelsea in January 2020 and was a key player in the final matches of the 2019-20 season.

Guehi was responsible for one of the stand-out moments of the Swans' dramatic surge into the Play-Off places, making a brilliant late block in the win over Reading. He rejoined on loan for the 2020-21 season.

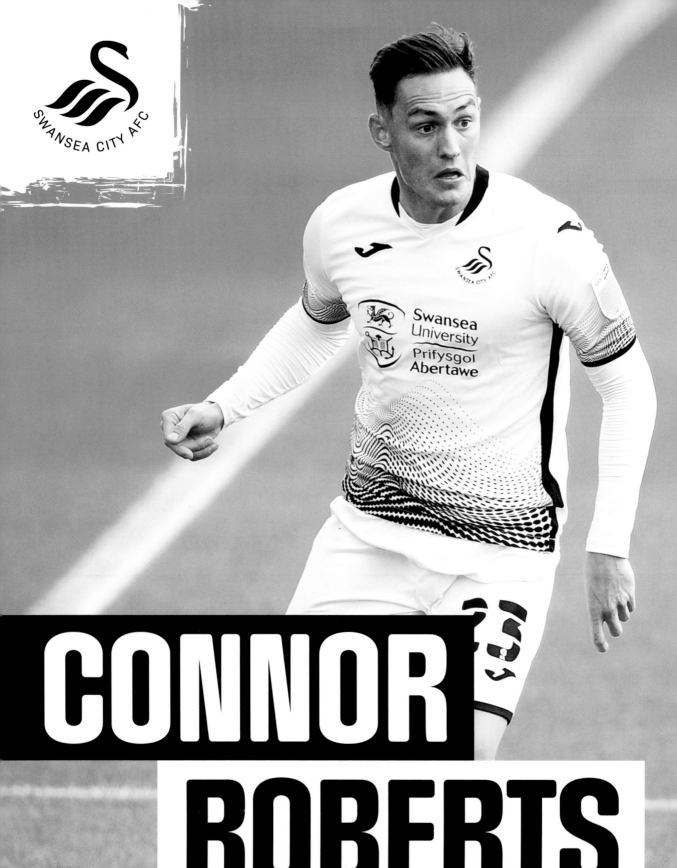

CONNOR
ROBERTS

SOCCER SKILLS

Great goalkeepers are an essential ingredient for successful teams in today's game. They have to excel in all areas of the art of 'keeping and Freddie Woodman is a great keeper that lives up to these expectations.

DISTRIBUTION

THE BASICS OF GOOD THROWING TECHNIQUE

OVERARM THROW

This is best for covering long distances. The body should be in line with the direction of the throw with the weight on the back foot. The ball should be brought forward in a bowling action with the arm straight.

JAVELIN THROW

This throw is made quickly with a low trajectory. The arm is bent for this throw, the ball is held beside the head and the body is in line with the direction of the throw. The arm is brought forward in a pushing movement with the ball being released at the top.

UNDERARM THROW

The ball is released from a crouching position, with a smooth underarm swing.

Throws do not usually travel as far as kicks but the greater speed and accuracy of throwing can make up for the lack of distance and will help the team retain possession. A player receiving a throw must be able to control it early.

Work hard at distribution and the benefits of this will be seen whenever you are in possession during a match.

EXERCISE ONE

Grab a friend and throw the ball to each other using the various throwing techniques at various distances apart.

EXERCISE TWO

The goalkeeper with the ball uses the various throws to knock another ball off a marker.

EXERCISE THREE

The goalkeepers try to throw the ball through the markers using various throwing techniques.

BOYS OF 1981

Etched into the history books of Swansea City is the date 1981. For this was the year the Swans became a top-flight team for the first time since the club's inception in 1912.

Promotion under John Toshack was the latest achievement under the guidance of the former Liverpool striker, who delivered three promotions in four seasons at the Vetch. He did so utilising a number of local lads who wore the Swansea crest with pride, with Toshack also showing his credentials as a young player-manager.

The all-important result came at Preston, where the hosts needed victory to avoid relegation while victory for the Swans would ensure them of a place in Division One.

Goals from Leighton James, Tommy Craig and Jeremy Charles were enough to send the Swans soaring into the top flight for the first time.

A superb debut season in Division One eventually ended with the team in sixth, with Toshack's men topping the table late on in the campaign before a slide in results

KEY MAN
LEIGHTON JAMES

While Toshack, as manager, could be a contender for being named the key man, local lad Leighton James proved a pivotal figure on the pitch.

Signed from Burnley, James' first season for his hometown club proved one to remember.

The winger ended the campaign as top scorer with 18 goals to his name,

His iconic strike against Preston on the final day helped the Swans on their way to promotion thanks to a 3-1 win.

JAY 6
FULTON

POSITION: Midfielder   **DOB:** 01/04/1994
COUNTRY: Scotland

Fulton joined the Swans from Falkirk in January 2014 and made his Premier League debut against Aston Villa three months later.

Last season, the Scot made 39 appearances for the Swans and netted three goals along the way. He made his 100th Swans appearance in the Championship Play-Off semi-final against Brentford at the Liberty in July.

7 KOREY SMITH

POSITION: Midfielder **DOB:** 31/01/1991
COUNTRY: England

Smith joined the Swans in the summer of 2020 after six years with Bristol City. The former Bristol City captain brought a lot of experience to Steve Cooper's side, having made over 170 Championship appearances in his career.

He made his Swans competitive debut in the Carabao Cup tie against Newport County at Rodney Parade in September.

MATT 8 GRIMES

POSITION: Midfielder **DOB:** 15/07/1995
COUNTRY: England

Swans captain Grimes joined the club in January 2015 from Exeter City. After a number of loan spells, he thrived during the 2018-19 season, making 50 appearances and picking up four separate awards in the end-of-season awards.

He played every minute of Swansea's 2019-20 league season and racked up his 100th Swans appearance in the win against Birmingham in July.

GOAL OF THE SEASON

WAYNE ROUTLEDGE

22 JULY 2020 — V READING

Wayne Routledge's magnificent lofted finish on the final day of the regular season at Reading was voted Goal of the Season by the Jack Army following the 2019-20 campaign.

The Swans entered the final game of the season knowing they had to beat Reading at the Madejski Stadium, but they would also need help from elsewhere.

Cardiff and Nottingham Forest were their two rivals, both three points ahead of the Swans. A defeat for either of those sides would open the door for Swansea, although they would also need a minimum goal difference swing of five in their favour if they were to overtake Forest.

The evening got off to a good start as the Swans were the first of the trio of Play-Off hopefuls to register a goal as Rhian Brewster smashed in a fantastic long-range strike. The Swans soon suffered a setback as George Puscas levelled from the spot.

With Forest's match back on level terms, Routledge gave Swansea hope as he superbly controlled a lovely pass from Matt Grimes and lofted the ball over Rafael Cabral and into the net.

Stoke were soon leading 3-1 at the City Ground, meaning the Swans only required two more goals to overtake Forest to reach the Play-Offs. They put themselves within tantalising reach when Liam Cullen, not long on the field as a substitute, superbly converted a half-volley to score his first senior goal.

Before Routledge headed home his second of the match in added time and the Swans were in the Play-Offs.

THE RUNNERS-UP

RHIAN BREWSTER V READING

The first runner-up with 36% of the vote was Rhian Brewster's long-range strike, also on the final day of the regular season against Reading at the Madejski.

Brewster picked the ball up some 30 yards out before smashing his 10th goal of the season that completely deceived Rafael in goal.

RHIAN BREWSTER V FOREST

Rhian Brewster emphatically smashed home his ninth goal of the season as the Swans were held to a 2-2 draw against Nottingham Forest at the City Ground.

Conor Gallagher laid the ball off for Jake Bidwell to deliver a ball that Brewster flashed home with a left-foot volley.

Challenge your favourite grown-up and find out which of you is the biggest Championship brain!

ADULTS

SWANSEA CITY AFC

Who is the only Championship club to have won the Premier League?

1 ANSWER

How many teams in the 2020/21 Championship have never competed in the Premier League?

2 ANSWER

Which former Leeds United and Norwich City midfielder currently plays for Middlesbrough?

3 ANSWER

At which Scottish club was QPR manager Mark Warburton once in charge?

4 ANSWER

Blackburn Rovers' manager Tony Mowbray previously played for and managed which Championship rival?

5 ANSWER

BLACKPOOL FOOTBALL CLUB

At which club did Sheffield Wednesday manager Garry Monk begin his managerial career?

6 ANSWER

From which club did Boro sign striker Britt Assombalonga?

7 ANSWER

Millwall manager Gary Rowett previously played for the Lions - true or false?

8 ANSWER

At which Championship ground will you find the Invincibles Stand?

9 ANSWER

In which year did Steve Cooper become Swansea City manager?

10 ANSWER

V KIDS

The adults' questions are on the left page and the kids' questions are on the right page.

Which Championship club play their home games at Carrow Road?

1 ANSWER

What is Sheffield Wednesday's nickname?

2 ANSWER

Which two clubs won automatic promotion to the Championship in 2019/20?

3 ANSWER

Ashton Gate is home to which Championship club?

4 ANSWER

Who is the manager of Cardiff City?

5 ANSWER

How many Welsh clubs are competing in the 2020/21 Championship?

6 ANSWER

Mark Warburton is the manager of which Championship team?

7 ANSWER

Which Championship stadium has the largest capacity?

8 ANSWER

How many Championship clubs have the word 'City' in their name?

9 ANSWER

What nationality is Preston manager Alex Neil?

10 ANSWER

ANSWERS ON PAGE 62

SWANSEA CITY AFC

Fill the page with your footy goals and dreams, no matter how big or small, and then start working on how to accomplish them!

We've started you off...

1. Visit the Liberty Stadium

2. Complete 50 keepy-uppies

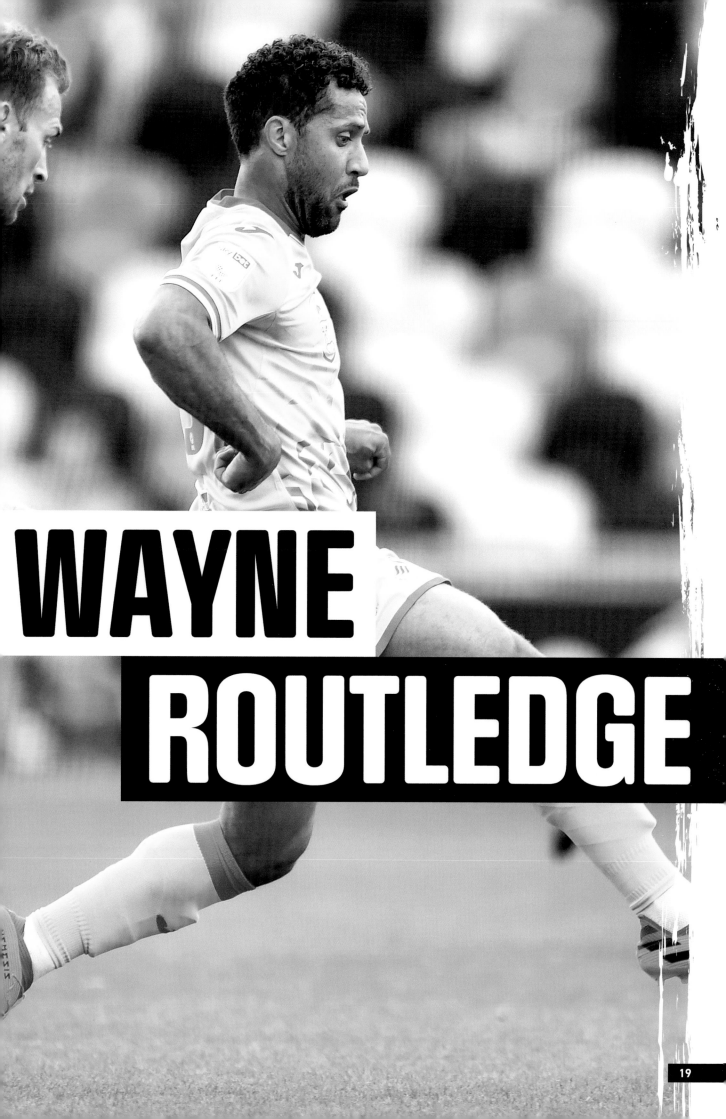

WAYNE
ROUTLEDGE

SWANSEA CITY AFC

1

2

3

4

5

20

ANSWERS ON PAGE 6

WHO ARE YER?

Can you figure out the identity of all these Swans stars?

6
7
8
9
10

JAMAL 9
LOWE

POSITION: Attacker **DOB:** 21/07/1994
COUNTRY: England

Winger Jamal Lowe joined the Swans from Wigan Athletic in August 2020. He featured in all of the Latics' 46 Championship games in 2019-20 before making the switch to Swansea.

He made his competitive debut for the Swans in the side's Carabao Cup clash against Newport County at Rodney Parade in September.

10 ANDRE
AYEW

POSITION: Attacker **DOB:** 17/12/1989
COUNTRY: Ghana

The Swans re-signed Ayew from West Ham in a club-record deal in January 2018. Last season, the Ghanaian was the club's top scorer after netting 18 goals in 47 appearances in all competitions.

He also picked up the Away Player of the Season, Players' Player of the Season and Supporters' player of the season accolades at the end of the campaign.

SWANSEA CITY AFC

MORGAN 11
GIBBS-WHITE

POSITION: Midfielder **DOB:** 27/01/2000
COUNTRY: England

The Swans completed the signing of Gibbs-White on a season-long loan from Wolverhampton Wanderers in August 2020.

The attacking midfielder had previously worked with head coach Steve Cooper in the England age-grade set-up as the Three Lions won the Under-17 World Cup in 2017. He made his competitive Swans debut against Newport County in the Carabao Cup in September.

PREPARING
FOR ACTION

ootball matches may
vell be scheduled for 90
ninutes but there are
nany days of preparation
hat go into making sure
hat Steve Cooper's men are at their
hysical and mental peak when they cross
he white line to represent Swansea City.

ike all Championship clubs, the Swans' pre-match planning
meticulous. The manager of course has final say as to who
nakes his starting line-up but the boss is ably assisted by
backroom staff of coaches, sports scientists, strength and
onditioning experts, physiotherapists and nutritionists who
ll play their part in helping fine tune the players ahead of
he manager's team selection.

he majority of the squads' preparations take place at the
lub's training ground and that all begins when the players
eport back for pre-season training.

Although the modern-day player has little
lown-time in terms of maintaining his overall
itness, pre-season really is a vital time for
ootballers to build themselves up to remain
s fit, strong and healthy as possible for the
hallenging season that awaits.

he pre-season schedule often begins with a series of fitness
ests. The results of those tests enables the club's coaching

and fitness staff to assess each player's condition and
level of fitness to ensure they are given the right work
load during the pre-season programme.

When it comes to winning football matches,
it is well known that both hard work and
practice are two essential ingredients to
success. However, in terms of strength and
fitness, then rest, recovery and diet also have
crucial parts to play in a footballer's wellbeing.

The modern game now sees technology playing its
part in training too - prior to beginning their training
sessions, the players are provided with a GPS tracking
system and heart rate analysis monitors ensuring that
all that they do in a training session can be measured,
monitored and reviewed.

**On-pitch training drills and gym work is
now enhanced further with players often
taking part in yoga and pilates classes
while always receiving expert advice in
terms of their diet, rest and mental
welfare.**

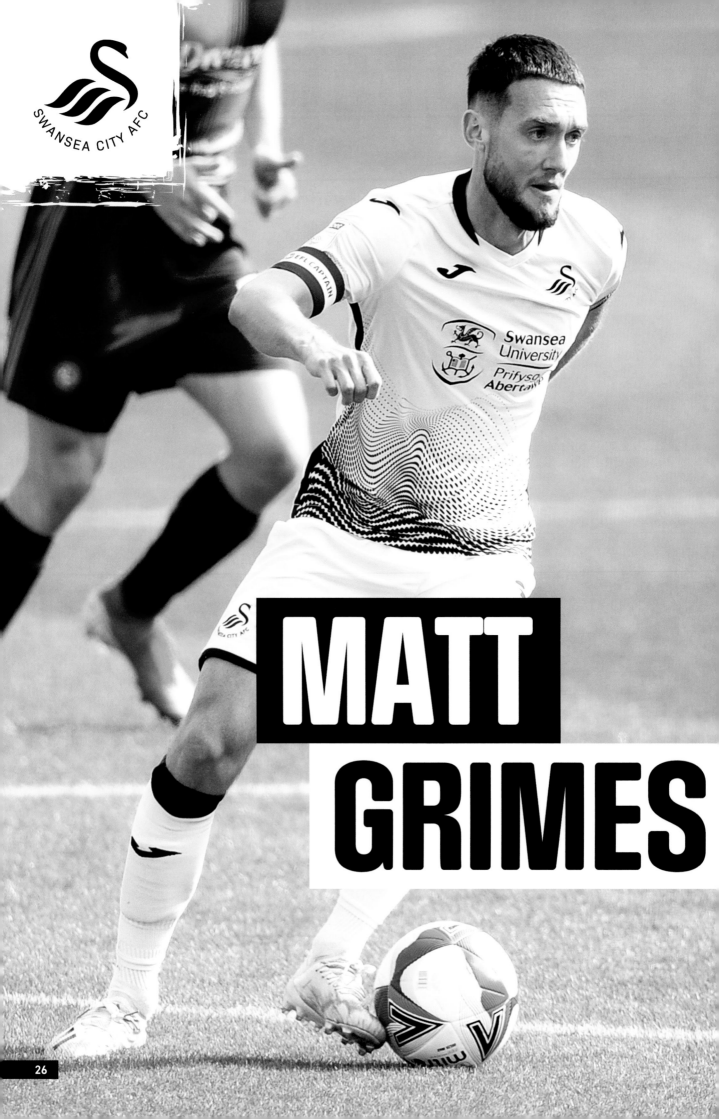

MATT
GRIMES

SOCCER SKILLS

DEFENDING

Defending is an art - not as spectacular as swerving a free kick around the wall into the net or floating a crossfield pass into the path of an oncoming wingback - but nevertheless, just as important. Every successful team has a solid defence and can defend as a team.

Defenders must also master the art of defending one on one...

EXERCISE ONE

Two adjacent 10m x 10m grids have two players, X and Y at the opposite ends of the grids. X plays the ball to Y, who is then allowed to attack defender X with the ball. Y's target is to be able to stop the ball, under control, on the opposite end line. Defender X has to try to stop this happening. Y is encouraged to be direct and run at X with the ball.

KEY FACTORS

1. Do not approach the attacker square on. Adopt a sideways stance which enables rapid forward and backwards movement.

2. Do not dive in. Be patient and wait for your opponent to make a mistake. Always be on your toes.

3. Threaten the ball without actually committing to a tackle. Pretending to tackle can often panic the opponent!

4. Tackle when you are sure you will win it!

EXERCISE TWO

Here the game is progressed to a two v two situation when X1 and X2 play as a team against Y1 and Y2.

The same target is used for this game - the players have to stand on the opposite line with the ball, either by dribbling past their opponents or by passing the ball through them.

The same key factors are relevant here with the addition of two more:

5. Covering your defending partner when he is being attacked.

6. Communication between the two defenders is vital.

If a team can get these points of defending right, throughout the side, they will become very difficult to beat.

SWANSEA CITY AFC

Take our quick-fire personality test to see where Steve Cooper would utilise your skills in the Swans line-up...

WHICH FOOTBALLER ARE YOU?

1. What is your favourite activity at the park?

a. Leaping around
b. Practicing my heading
c. Lots of non-stop running
d. Scoring goals

2. What is your biggest strength?

a. My height
b. My strength
c. My stamina
d. My speed

3. Which would you rather win?

a. A game of catch
b. A weight lifting contest
c. A long distance run
d. A sprint race

4. You score a goal! How do you celebrate?

a. I turn and punch the air
b. I clench my fist in delight
c. I high-five a teammate
d. I slide on my knees

5. How would the opposition describe you?

a. Hard to beat
b. Determined to succeed
c. All-action
d. Lethal in front of goal

6. What's your favourite move?

a. Springing high to catch under pressure
b. A sliding tackle
c. Playing the perfect through ball
d. Spinning away from my marker

7. What is the key to winning a game?

a. Keeping a clean sheet

b. Winning your individual battles

c. Maintaining possession

d. Taking chances that come your way

8. What is your favourite number?

a. One

b. Five

c. Seven

d. Nine

9. How would you describe your style of play?

a. Disciplined

b. Fully committed

c. Relentless

d. Technically gifted

10. What do your teammates call you?

a. Secure

b. Reliable

c. Energetic

d. Mr/Miss goals

MOSTLY As

You would clearly be a safe pair of hands in goal. Watch out Freddie Woodman, there's competition for the No1 shirt!

MOSTLY Bs

Sounds like you are a young Joe Rodon in the making - there could well be a role for you in the Swans back four...

MOSTLY Cs

You could comfortably take your place in the heart of midfield and help make things tick at Liberty Stadium. Move over Korey Smith!

MOSTLY Ds

Looks like we have a budding Jamal Lowe on our hands! Who do you fancy partnering in attack?

STEVEN 13
BENDA

POSITION: Goalkeeper   **DOB:** 01/10/1998
COUNTRY: Germany

Benda joined Swansea from 1860 Munich on a three-year deal in August 2017. He earned himself the reputation as a 'penalty killer', notably saving two penalties in the FAW Youth Cup final in 2018.

Benda had a successful loan spell at Swindon Town in the 2019-20 season and is now involved in Steve Cooper's first-team squad after signing a new deal through to June 2022.

VIKTOR 14
GYÖKERES

POSITION: Striker   **DOB:** 04/06/1998
COUNTRY: Sweden

Gyökeres joined the Swans on a season-long loan from Brighton & Hove Albion in October 2020 and made his debut the following day as a substitute against Millwall at the Liberty.

The Swedish international has won two caps for his country and spent the 2019-20 season on loan at St Pauli in the German second tier.

TEAM 2020/21

SWANSEA CITY AFC

WAYNE 15
ROUTLEDGE

POSITION: Midfielder   **DOB:** 07/01/1985
COUNTRY: England

**Approaching a decade of service, Routledge
extended his stay with the Swans after signing
a new one-year deal last summer.**

He joined the Swans from Newcastle in 2011 and
has gone on to make over 280 appearances. He
scored a vital goal against Reading in the 2019-20
season to help the Swans earn a place in the
Championship Play-Offs.

BOYS OF

2011

For the first time in the club's history, Swansea City were now a Premier League club.

Just eight years after being just 90 minutes away from dropping into non-league football, the Swans were now sitting at the top table of English football.

Brendan Rodgers had taken over as manager in the summer of 2010, and his first season at the Liberty brought the ultimate reward.

Continuing to build on the football legacy left by Roberto Martinez and adding to the work put in by Paulo Sousa, Rodgers guided the Swans to the Promised Land.

After a third-placed finish in the Championship, the Swans faced Nottingham Forest in the semi-finals. Following a 0-0 draw at the City Ground, despite the dismissal of Neil Taylor in the second minute, the Swans saw off Forest 3-1 at a charged-up

SCOTT SINCLAIR

With 27 goals in his debut season, there is no doubting Scott Sinclair's impact in SA1.

The winger, signed from Chelsea, made an incredible impact under Rodgers as Sinclair turned potential into end product.

He proved a nightmare for opposing full-backs, who simply could not deal with his pace and directness.

Of his 27 goals, a certain hat-trick at Wembley proved the most important. Sinclair stepped up to the plate and put in one of his best performances of the campaign as two penalties and another strike sunk Reading as the Swans booked their place in the Premier League.

Liberty which witnessed one of the stadium's finest atmospheres.

That win meant the Jack Army were heading to Wembley, where the Swans faced Rodgers' former club Reading in the final.

Having raced into a 3-0 lead at the break, the Swans were pegged back to 3-2 before captain Garry Monk made one of the most famous blocks in the club's history to deny Reading a certain equaliser.

From there, the Swans never looked back as Scott Sinclair sealed victory and promotion late on from the penalty spot as he claimed a hat-trick. Victory meant the Swans became the first Welsh club to be promoted to the Premier League, with the team celebrating in front of 40,000 Jacks.

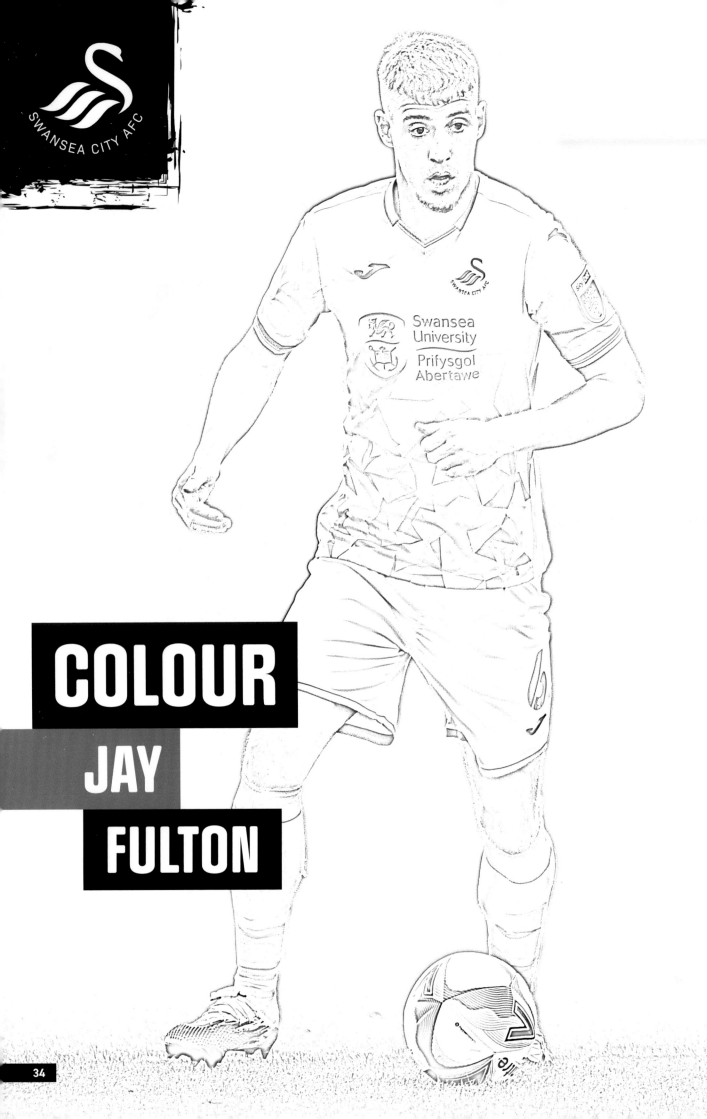

SWANSEA CITY AFC

COLOUR
JAY
FULTON

34

ANDRE
AYEW

PLAYER OF THE SEASON

ANDRE AYEW

Voted both Supporters' Player of the Year and Players' Player of the Year, Andre Ayew enjoyed a superb year, netting 18 goals in all competitions and setting up seven more as he helped Steve Cooper's side reach the Championship Play-Offs.

Ayew's season was full of inspirational displays and memorable moments, ranging from his superb assists for Bersant Celina and Sam Surridge in a win at QPR, a late winner at Luton and a simply stunning strike to sink Brentford in the first leg of the Play-Off semi-final.

The Ghanaian opened his account in the Swans' first game of the 2019-20 season, netting twice as Steve Cooper's men defeated Northampton Town 3-1 at the Liberty.

He netted the winner away to Charlton in October before finding the net in the following two matches against Stoke and Barnsley respectively.

Ayew scored another six before the end of the calendar year, including an 82nd-minute winner at Kenilworth Road to seal three points for the Liberty club away to Luton.

The winner at home to Wigan and goals against Huddersfield and Blackburn followed before the season was curtailed due to the Coronavirus pandemic.

Following the resumption of the season, the vice-captain was in fine form and made an impressive impact in the club's push for a top-six finish and found the net against Middlesbrough, Sheffield Wednesday, Nottingham Forest and the Play-Off semi-final against Brentford.

YOUNG PLAYER OF THE SEASON

TIVONGE RUSHESHA

The Under-23s' Player of the Season was full-back Tivonge Rushesha, who was one of a number of young players to make their first-team debut over the season.

Rushesha was an impressive performer and regularly featured in defence for the development side whilst he also became one of the youngest-ever players to appear for Swansea City's first team when he featured as a substitute in the Carabao Cup win over Cambridge United at the age of just 17 years and 35 days old.

The Wales Under-17 international's efforts were rewarded with a first professional contract in January 2020, keeping him at the club until the summer of 2022.

LIAM **20** CULLEN

POSITION: Attacker   **DOB:** 23/04/1999
COUNTRY: Wales

Part of the Swans academy since he was eight years old, Cullen scored ten goals for the under-23s during the 2018-19 season.

He was just 13 when he made his debut for the under-18s, and made his first-team bow against Crystal Palace in 2018. The Welshman netted his first senior goal in the crucial final-day win at Reading last season.

21 YAN DHANDA

POSITION: Midfielder   **DOB:** 14/12/1998
COUNTRY: England

Attacking midfielder Dhanda joined the club in May 2018 after two-and-a-half years with Liverpool and scored the winning goal at Sheffield United just 29 seconds into his Swans debut.

He made 19 appearances in the 2019-20 season and scored three goals along the way, including the winner in the club's 1-0 home victory over Charlton in January.

CONNOR 23 ROBERTS

POSITION: Defender   **DOB:** 23/09/1995
COUNTRY: Wales

Wales international Roberts came through the club's academy before earning himself a professional contract.

The right-back played 42 times for the Swans in the 2019-20 season, racking up his 100th Swans appearance in the crucial victory at Reading on the final day of the regular campaign. Roberts' incredible stamina and energy has become a regular fixture down the Swans' right flank.

There are five Cyril the Swans hiding in the crowd as Swansea fans celebrate winning the League Cup in 2013. Can you find him?

ANSWERS ON PAGE 62

CLASSIC
FANTASTIC

SWANSEA CITY AFC

JAMAL
LOWE

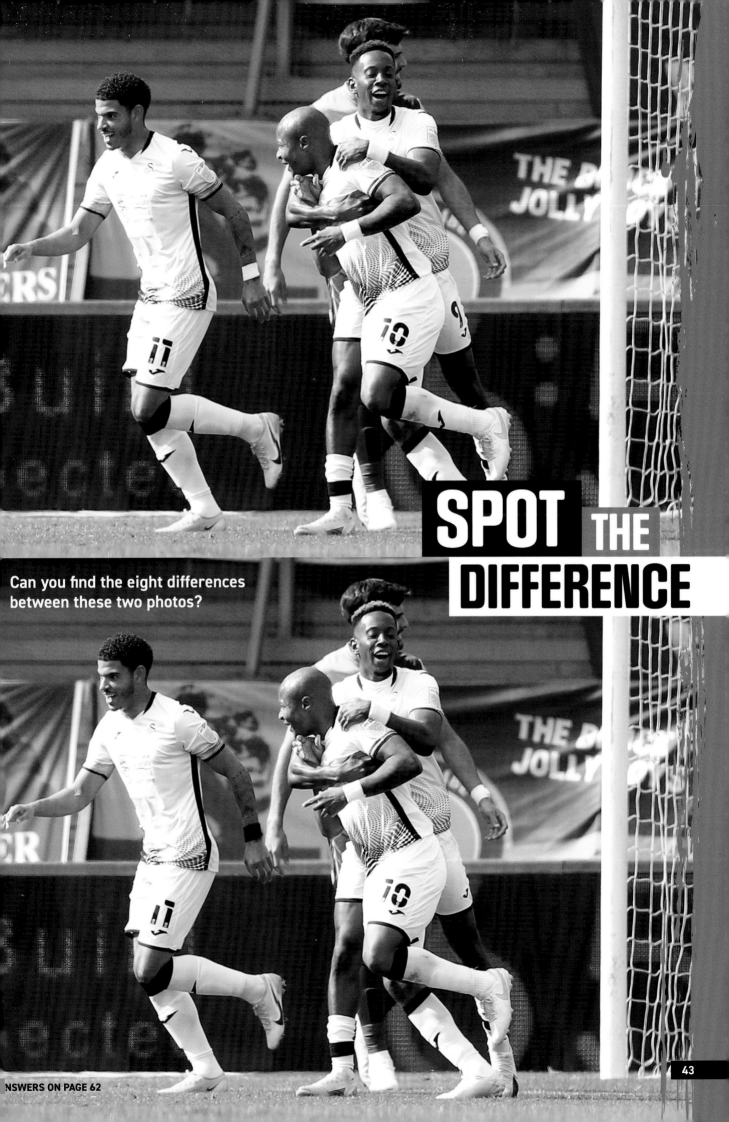

SPOT THE DIFFERENCE

Can you find the eight differences between these two photos?

NSWERS ON PAGE 62

2020/21

PREMIER LEAGUE

OUR PREDICTION FOR PREMIER LEAGUE WINNERS:

LEICESTER CITY

YOUR PREDICTION:

OUR PREDICTION FOR PREMIER LEAGUE RUNNERS-UP:

LIVERPOOL

YOUR PREDICTION:

CHAMPIONSHIP

OUR PREDICTION FOR CHAMPIONSHIP WINNERS:

SWANSEA CITY

YOUR PREDICTION:

OUR PREDICTION FOR CHAMPIONSHIP RUNNERS-UP:

MIDDLESBROUGH

YOUR PREDICTION:

TOP SCORERS

OUR PREDICTION FOR PREMIER LEAGUE TOP SCORER:
PIERRE-EMERICK AUBAMEYANG

YOUR PREDICTION:

OUR PREDICTION FOR CHAMPIONSHIP TOP SCORER:
ANDRE AYEW

YOUR PREDICTION:

FA CUP & EFL CUP

OUR PREDICTION FOR FA CUP WINNERS:
WATFORD

YOUR PREDICTION:

OUR PREDICTION FOR EFL CUP WINNERS:
BRIGHTON & HA

YOUR PREDICTION:

PREDICTIONS

24 JAKE
BIDWELL

POSITION: Defender **DOB:** 21/03/1993
COUNTRY: England

Bidwell arrived at Swansea in the summer of 2019 on a free transfer following a successful three-year spell at QPR.

In his first season as a Swan, the left-back made 40 appearances and helped the side reach the Championship Play-Offs. After starting the season operating as a left-back, Bidwell was deployed as a wing-back towards the end of last season.

KYLE 26
NAUGHTON

POSITION: Defender **DOB:** 17/11/1988
COUNTRY: England

Naughton joined the Swans from Tottenham in January 2015 and has featured at full-back, wing-back, centre-back and in the heart of midfield.

He signed a new one-year contract in August 2020 to extend his Liberty Stadium stay by a further 12 months. He has netted six goals in over 180 appearances, including strikes against Birmingham, Derby and Hull in the 2019-20 season.

GEORGE 28
BYERS

POSITION: Midfielder **DOB:** 29/05/1996
COUNTRY: England

After 13 years at Watford, Byers joined the Swans in July 2016. Byers was named Swans under-23s Player of the Season in 2017-18 after scoring ten goals and making nine assists.

He made his Swans senior debut against Crystal Palace in the Carabao Cup in August 2018. Last season, Byers made 39 Swans appearances, scoring five goals.

MORGAN GIBBS-WHITE

SOCCER SKILLS
CHEST CONTROL

Controlling the ball quickly and with minimum fuss in order to get the ball where you want it, so you can pass or shoot, can be the difference between a good player and a top class player.

EXERCISE ONE

Grab two of your mates to start the exercise. A and C stand 10yds apart and have a ball each, ready to act as servers.

B works first. B must run towards A who serves the ball for B to control with the chest and pass back to A. B then turns, runs to C and repeats the exercise.

Once B has worked for 30 seconds all the players rotate.

KEY FACTORS

1. Look to control the ball as early as possible.
2. Get in line with the ball.
3. Keep eyes on the ball.
4. Relax the body on impact with the ball to cushion it.

EXERCISE TWO

In this exercise there are 5 servers positioned around a 15yd square. At one side of the square there is a goal.

T starts in the middle of the square. S1 serves first, throwing the ball in the air towards T. T must control the ball with the chest and try to shoot past the goalkeeper, as soon as T has shot on goal they must prepare for the next serve from S2.

Once T has received a ball from every server the players rotate positions - the same key factors apply.

Players who can control a ball quickly, putting the ball in a position for a shot or pass, give themselves and their teammates the extra valuable seconds required in today's intense style of play.

Challenge your favourite grown-up and find out which of you is the biggest Championship brain!

ADULTS

11 Prior to moving to the Madejski Stadium, where did Reading play their home matches?

ANSWER

12 Which kit manufacturer produces Queens Park Rangers' 2020/21 playing strip?

ANSWER

13 At which Championship club did Preston goalkeeper Declan Rudd begin his career?

ANSWER

14 What nationality is Millwall goalkeeper Bartosz Bialkowski?

ANSWER

15 At which club did Coventry City manager Mark Robins begin his managerial career?

ANSWER

16 Who did Garry Monk succeed as Sheffield Wednesday boss in 2019?

ANSWER

17 What was the name of Derby County's former ground?

ANSWER

18 Cardiff City midfielder Will Vaulks plays international football for which country?

ANSWER

19 Who is the captain of Stoke City?

ANSWER

20 From which club did Preston North End sign Scott Sinclair?

ANSWER

50

V KIDS

The adults' questions are on the left page and the kids' questions are on the right page.

NSWERS ON PAGE 62

Who is the manager of Reading?

11 ANSWER

Wayne Rooney plays for which Championship club?

12 ANSWER

With which country is Norwich goalkeeper Tim Krul a full international?

13 ANSWER

Which club's nickname is 'The Lions'?

14 ANSWER

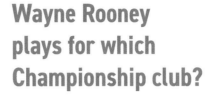

Which country did Stoke City manager Michael O'Neill guide to finals of Euro 2016?

15 ANSWER

What nationality is Norwich City manager Daniel Farke?

16 ANSWER

Rammie and Ewie are the official mascots of which Championship club?

17 ANSWER

Queens Park Rangers are famous for playing in what type of shirts?

18 ANSWER

Which Championship team play their home matches at Ewood Park?

19 ANSWER

Who is the manager of Rotherham United?

20 ANSWER

BOYS OF 2013

Quite simply, the finest year in the Swans' history.

When the Great Dane Michael Laudrup was appointed manager in 2012, something special was brewing.

And that culminated in a 2013 that Swans fans will forever cherish as they lifted the League Cup.

The club's major trophy saw the likes of holders Liverpool and Chelsea disposed of on route to the final, where they beat Bradford City by a record final score of 5-0 at Wembley.

While the results were memorable, the style of football played under Laudrup also caught the eye as The Swansea Way was at it's peak.

A ninth-placed finish in the Premier League - then a club record position in the division - was accomplished, while their cup success meant a European adventure.

The highlight came via a 3-0 win over Spaniards Valencia at the iconic Mestalla, while the journey ended in the round of 32 at the hands of Napoli.

KEY MAN

MICHU

While the Swans won plenty of plaudits for their success, there was no doubting who their main man was.

Spanish star Michu played a key role that season, scoring 22 goals in all competitions as Laudrup's men finished ninth in the Premier League.

A bargain £2million signing from Rayo Vallecano, Michu marked his debut with a stunning two-goal performance in an opening-day demolition of QPR, while he would also bag a brace as the Swans recorded a memorable 2-0 win over Arsenal at the Emirates.

His performances for his club were rewarded by his country as Michu would become the first Swan to be capped by Spain.

TIVONGE 30
RUSHESHA

POSITION: Defender   **DOB:** 24/07/2002
COUNTRY: Wales

Zimbabwe-born Rushesha has gone from strength to strength after joining the Swans academy at under-12 level.

He became a regular in the under-23s squad and at the age of just 17 years and 35 days old, Rushesha became one of the youngest-ever players to appear for the Swans' first team as a substitute in the Carabao Cup win over Cambridge.

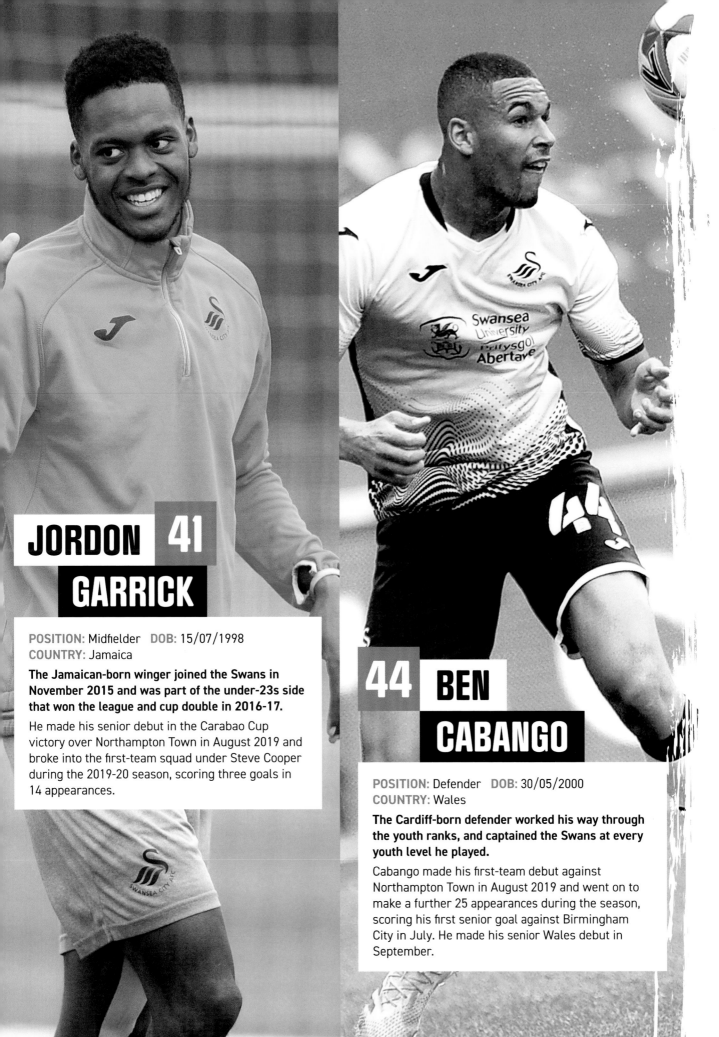

JORDON 41
GARRICK

POSITION: Midfielder **DOB:** 15/07/1998
COUNTRY: Jamaica

The Jamaican-born winger joined the Swans in November 2015 and was part of the under-23s side that won the league and cup double in 2016-17.

He made his senior debut in the Carabao Cup victory over Northampton Town in August 2019 and broke into the first-team squad under Steve Cooper during the 2019-20 season, scoring three goals in 14 appearances.

44 BEN
CABANGO

POSITION: Defender **DOB:** 30/05/2000
COUNTRY: Wales

The Cardiff-born defender worked his way through the youth ranks, and captained the Swans at every youth level he played.

Cabango made his first-team debut against Northampton Town in August 2019 and went on to make a further 25 appearances during the season, scoring his first senior goal against Birmingham City in July. He made his senior Wales debut in September.

Here is a list of footy jargon. All but one of the terms are hidden in the grid...

...can you work out which is missing?

All To Play For

Back Of The Net

Bags Of Pace

Big Game Player

Box-To-Box

Class Act

Derby Day

Dinked In

Early Doors

Funny Old Game

Game Of Two Halves

Handbags

Hat-Trick

Hollywood Pass

Keep It Tight

Massive Game

Midfield General

Natural Goalscorer

Row Z

Worldy

A	S	M	Z	U	C	E	M	A	G	E	V	I	S	S	A	M
V	A	W	T	B	X	O	W	A	C	V	T	S	V	Y	B	N
P	O	I	B	Y	D	I	N	K	E	D	I	N	B	R	Q	A
R	L	Q	C	J	K	X	Z	E	F	M	L	F	J	N	E	T
O	G	F	W	K	C	I	R	T	T	A	H	C	S	A	Z	U
E	X	B	H	D	A	V	A	P	N	H	X	G	B	J	E	R
T	K	A	L	L	T	O	P	L	A	Y	F	O	R	D	C	A
I	R	C	P	M	E	Q	M	O	L	R	X	G	H	O	A	L
F	L	K	D	N	U	R	A	S	T	T	P	K	Q	C	P	G
U	F	O	N	Z	Y	D	I	W	O	M	W	Y	I	B	F	O
N	H	F	W	Z	O	E	S	B	B	U	N	E	H	L	O	A
N	J	T	G	O	B	N	O	D	F	F	X	K	A	D	S	L
Y	Z	H	S	V	R	X	M	A	G	V	O	R	N	I	G	S
O	X	E	A	D	C	L	H	H	G	A	E	U	D	Z	A	C
L	B	N	K	Q	J	L	D	C	J	N	K	A	B	I	B	O
D	D	E	R	B	Y	D	A	Y	E	S	P	A	L	B	R
G	W	T	E	U	O	I	P	G	J	I	O	J	G	S	M	E
A	C	I	O	K	I	R	D	Y	U	X	K	T	S	F	A	R
M	H	W	V	Y	B	L	T	B	P	C	H	F	O	R	R	A
E	O	P	C	D	E	E	T	G	E	G	Q	B	L	P	E	N
V	G	C	M	I	H	A	F	M	I	E	K	Y	V	Z	G	L
H	J	B	F	D	W	A	R	T	X	I	D	H	D	C	T	D
L	X	D	M	O	A	S	T	A	S	O	L	G	A	T	C	R
V	I	A	Q	K	Y	I	H	S	O	D	W	J	H	Y	A	Q
M	P	F	E	Z	P	R	G	R	G	U	N	F	M	I	S	G
Z	I	N	Q	E	J	N	S	L	J	P	I	K	Z	Y	S	O
D	B	S	E	V	L	A	H	O	W	T	F	O	E	M	A	G
E	K	T	X	S	L	T	E	M	X	K	W	U	L	L	I
U	S	N	Q	L	U	W	E	A	B	V	R	S	P	C	O
A	Y	O	R	S	F	I	T	W	Y	O	T	A	N	B	M
H	O	L	L	Y	W	O	O	D	P	A	S	S	U	T	I

ANSWERS ON PAGE 6

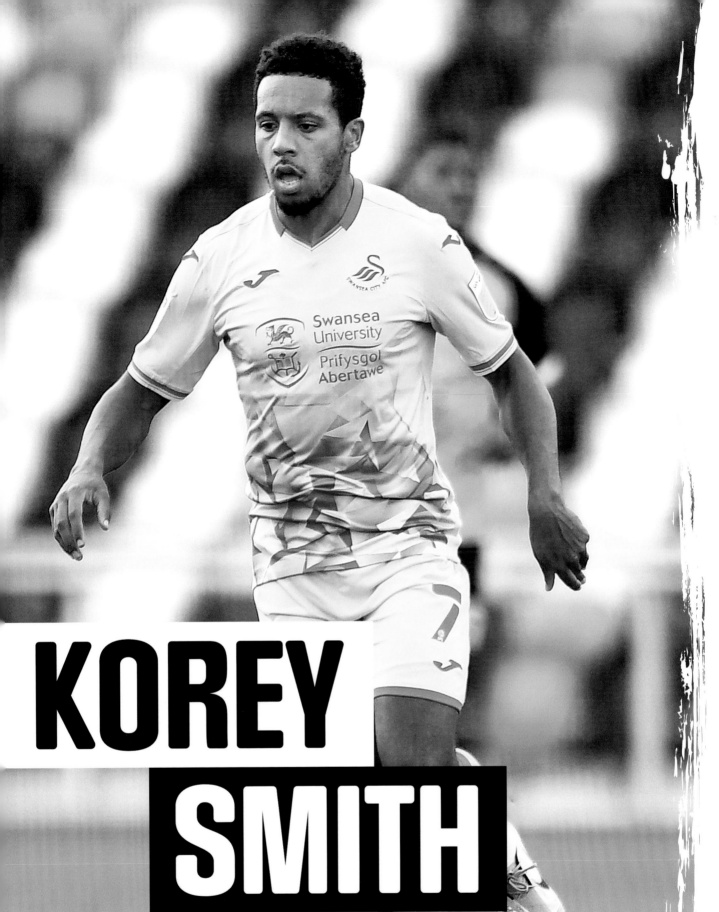

KOREY
SMITH

30 DAY

SWANSEA CITY AFC

Day 1
Right let's get started!
10 squats, 25 star jumps,
10 sit-ups - all
before school!

Day 2
Make your mum
a brew before going
out to practice your
keepy-uppys

Day 3
10 squats
50 star jumps
10 sit-ups

Day 4
How about swapping
the crisps in
your lunchbox
for an apple?

Day 5
Take a one
mile ride on
your bike

Day 6
75 star jumps
15 sit-ups
15 press-ups

Day 7
Help clean the
car before going out
to play headers and
volleys with your
friends

Day 8
75 star jumps
15 sit-ups
15 press-ups
Before and after school now!

Day 9
Walk to school
rather than
take the bus

Day 10
Head to the
swimming pool
for a 30-minute
swim

Day 11
100 star jumps
20 sit-ups
20 press-ups
Twice a day now,
don't forget!

Day 12
Make sure you trade
one of your fizzy
drinks for a glass
of water today

Day 13
Jog to the shop for
your mum... before
playing any video
games!

Day 14
Give a hand around the
house before kicking
your ball against the
wall 500 times

Day 15
Time to increase those exercises!
25 squats
25 sit-ups
25 press-ups
Before and after school!

Day 16
Take a nice paced two-mile jog today

Day 17
25 squats
150 star jumps
25 press-ups
Remember, before and after school

Day 18
Cycle to school rather than rely on the bus or a lift

Day 19
30 squats
150 star jumps
30 press-ups
Twice a day too!

Day 20
Get out and practice those free-kicks, practice makes perfect remember...

Day 21
Get peddling!
Time for a two-mile trip on two wheels today

Day 22
Upping the workload now...
40 squats, 40 sit-ups
40 press-ups
Before and after school!

Day 23
Wave goodbye to the chips - ask for a nice salad for lunch today

Day 24
40 squats
40 sit-ups
40 press-ups
Twice a day, don't forget...

Day 25
Time to get pounding the streets - the jogging is up to three miles today

Day 26
45 star jumps
45 sit-ups
45 press-ups

Day 27
Time to swap those sweets and biscuits for some fruit

Day 28
45 star jumps
45 sit-ups
45 press-ups

Day 29
You're getting fitter and fitter now! Keep up the squats and star jumps plus join an after-school sports club - ideally football!

Day 30
Well done - you made it!
50 squats, 50 sit-ups and 50 press-ups!
These are the core ingredients to your success

CHALLENGE
to improve your all-round footy fitness!

Can you figure out what ball is the real one in each photo?

WHAT BALL?

ANSWERS ON PAGE 61

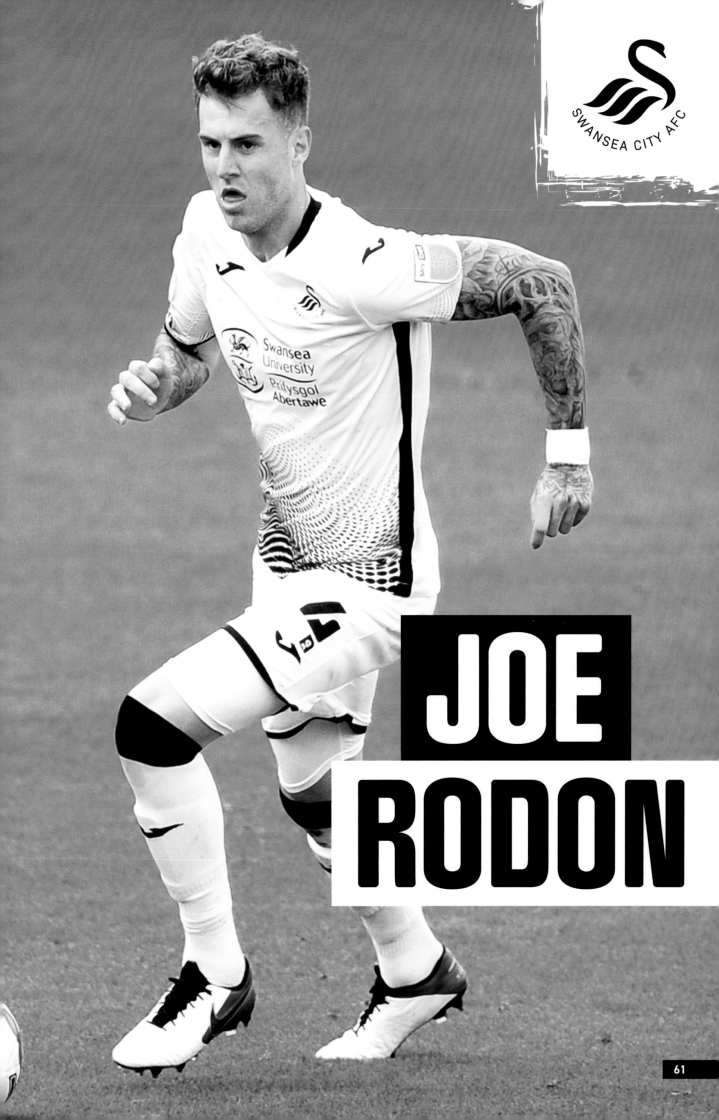

JOE
RODON

ANSWERS

PAGE 16 · ADULTS V KIDS

Adults

1. Blackburn Rovers. 2. Seven – Brentford, Bristol City, Luton Town, Millwall, Preston North End, Rotherham United and Wycombe Wanderers. 3. Jonny Howson. 4. Glasgow Rangers. 5. Middlesbrough. 6. Swansea City. 7. Nottingham Forest. 8. False. 9. Deepdale, Preston North End. 10. 2019.

Kids

1. Norwich City. 2. The Owls. 3. Coventry City and Rotherham United. 4. Bristol City. 5. Neil Harris. 6. Two, Cardiff City and Swansea City. 7. QPR. 8. Hillsborough, Sheffield Wednesday. 9. Seven - Birmingham City, Bristol City, Cardiff City, Coventry City, Norwich City, Stoke City and Swansea City. 10. Scottish.

PAGE 20 · WHO ARE YER?

1. Korey Smith. 2. Tivonge Rushesha.
3. Yan Dhanda. 4. Daniel Williams.
5. Jamal Lowe. 6. Morgan Gibbs-White.
7. Joe Rodon. 8. Wayne Routledge.
9. Matt Grimes. 10. Declan John.

PAGE 40
CLASSIC FANTASTIC →

PAGE 43
SPOT THE DIFFERENCE →

PAGE 50 · ADULTS V KIDS

Adults

11. Elm Park. 12. Errea. 13. Norwich City.
14. Polish. 15. Rotherham United. 16. Steve Bruce. 17. The Baseball Ground. 18. Wales.
19. Ryan Shawcross. 20. Celtic.

Kids

11. Veljko Paunović. 12. Derby County. 13. Holland.
14. Millwall. 15. Northern Ireland. 16. German.
17. Derby County. 18. Blue and white hoops.
19. Blackburn Rovers. 20. Paul Warne.

PAGE 56 · JARGON BUSTER

Big Game Player

PAGE 60 · WHAT BALL?

TOP: Ball D.
BOTTOM: Ball D.